"Chloe N. Clark deftly evolves and interrogates what it means to be a body moving through the mysterious expanse of space, getting lost in dark forests of emptiness but finding comfort in the stars, in the earth, in networks of roots. A Daphne figure, fleeing men, is turned into a tree, and the question is posed: 'Would you beg the gods / for some other kind of saving?' In this world, myths, spells, magic tricks, dreams, space travel, and forests constellate a rumination on how to transcend the threats and limitations of flesh and bone—as she writes, 'I wanted to be Houdini, be someone who escaped death over and over.' Clark conjures the cosmic rifts between us, grasping the loneliness and the inevitable losses of life, but her poems pivot on the hope of transformation: space can be an emptiness that 'holds you.' Trees push 'through our bones' and carry them skyward. A tree may die, but 'still cuttings from it / could be regrown, rerooted.' We may seek an escape from the body, but in these poems, we are reminded that sometimes 'the body can be a key.' In *Escaping the Body*, Clark beautifully binds hope to fear, shining light on the dark tableau of our present moment."

—Maegan Poland, author of *What Makes You Think You're Awake?*

" Part haunted mansion, part house of mirrors, part rocket ship, and always aching and honest, *Escaping the Body* plumbs the depths of what it is a poem can do and emerges with untold treasures. Who else could write a confessional poem turning PC error codes into ekphrastic vignettes? Or wreck us softly with the image of a sleepwalking lover weeping? Or make a love poem out of two people turning into sharks? This is a book of magic – of blood and cauldron and spell and tree, but also of straitjacket and lock to pick and risk of drowning, with Clark acting as both enchantress and Houdini."

—Todd Dillard, author of *The Ways We Vanish*

Escaping the Body

by Chloe N. Clark

This is a work of fiction. All of the characters, organizations, and events portrayed are either products of the author's imagination or used fictitiously.

ESCAPING THE BODY

Text Copyright © 2022 by Chloe N. Clark

Edited by Holly Lyn Walrath.
Cover design by Nana Masyuk-Frantsuzova.

Published by Interstellar Flight Press
Houston, Texas.
www.interstellarflightpress.com

Print ISBN: 978-1-953736-08-6
Ebook ISBN: 978-1-953736-09-3

First Edition: 2022

Escaping the Body

by Chloe N. Clark

Contents

Bullet Tricks

"A magician is an actor playing the part of a magician."
—Jean-Robert Houdin

Questions We Asked for the Girls Turned to Limbs

Do you remember the hands of men? How they pressed
into your skin until red blossomed
across the surface?
                    How their intentions left
patterns on your body? When you fled
through fields, through forests, up mountains,
up hills, into streams, into lakes
                    did you cry out for anyone?
Did your voice sound like bells even then?
If you turned into a tree, was it your choice
what kind it was? Did you choose on a whim or
                    was there a certain logic?
Willow because you weeped or pine because
of the smell? Do you remember how fast
the ones you loved gave up looking
                    for you? Was it gradual, the way
they lost hope? Or was it sudden: a violent
loss of faith? When you spent years rooted
to the ground, did it remind you of every time
                    you'd been rooted in place by fear?
Was it a curse more than a blessing?
If you could choose would you want to be something
other than a tree, other than locked into the
                    earth so fiercely?
Maybe a lake pebble that a fish might swallow? A feather?
Do you remember how your mother
braided your hair, even with hands full of aching? How she
                    smoothed the strands so gently?
How she always said 'you are
a lovely one' every time after? When you knew
you were lost, after the escape, the run, the change,
                    was there a moment
when you almost let go?
When you thought how easy
it would be? If you could, what would you do
                    differently?
Would you kiss your mother's hands?

Ask your father one more story?
Would you beg the gods
                    for some other kind of saving?

Dissolutions

My friend describes the bodies she works upon
        synthetic cadavers—designed to be perfect
recreations of muscles, bones, veins, such bodies
        which have never held breath.

                When I met you, you said you studied
                    the reactions of muscles
                the memories our bodies form—
                    you ran a finger along my arm,
                felt the tendons as I flexed, relaxed.

My friend says she used to be scared
        of them, the bodies laid out
on tables, bodies that had never held
        souls. She imagined what
they wanted, what they longed for,
        without ever having known longing or want.

                You once pressed the flat of your
                hands
                    over my body, found the
                points
                that made me arch my back, made me
                gasp,
                you said that you liked the wayI
                balanced on my toes to reach the top
                shelves,
                    the way I twirled a pen
                between two fingers,
                the clench of my jaw in pleasure

My friend goes through the list
        of how to care for a synthetic cadaver—
keep it hydrated, stored somewhere tightly
        closed, use a special chemical to keep
away algae, she says: imagine if we had to do
        that to ourselves?

You told me, on our last phone call, how
        you imagined life unfolding
like a phantom pain where muscles
        once grew—a memory that something
could hurt long after it was no longer there.

My friend says she's gotten used
        to the bodies, that she thinks
of them as dolls now, no longer
        as shells that are almost us.

You left yourself in pieces around my
        apartment—the indent of your body
in my bed, the fingerprints on the shower glass.

Missing Girl Found—

dead

or

missing girl found alive

or

missing girl found living in Paris, in New York City, in Rio de Janeiro, in Hollywood, in Wonewoc, Wisconsin, because she'd always appreciated alliteration

or

missing girl found to be unhelpful, psychics say, shaking their heads, "it's as if she doesn't want to be found"

or

missing girl found to be the last goddamn straw to woman who moves away because the town is turning, changing, becoming some place unrecognizable

or

missing girl found underwater

or

missing girl found to have been abducted by aliens, bandits, a coven of witches

or missing girl

found wanting

or

missing girl found to have been loved by her family and now her mother sometimes curls into her daughter's bed during the day, struggling to inhale her secrets, or even just the scent of her shampoo dug deep into pillows

or

missing girl found beautiful, years later, by someone seeing her photograph as they page through an old yearbook and know nothing of her except that she was beautiful

or

missing girl found seven years later, released from faerie and imagining nothing has changed

or

missing girl found to have kept a dream journal, the last entry:
I was underwater, at first scared, and then knew, somehow,
I was meant to be there, I was part of the water,

the river,
the rush that keeps it moving
                    or
missing girl found to have never existed at all
                    or
missing girl found to be happy
          or
missing girl found to be missed
                    or
                    or
                    or

It's the Horror of My Friends that We Say Mean Things about Blondes

We curl our lips above our teeth, snarls
to show that we mean it
and we count off all the ones
we've let go of:
sometimes we can't even remember
their names, the color of their eyes,
the sounds they made in pleasure

when people say our names,
we don't always answer
because giving in to a name
is being devoured by it,
we like it best when you
scream it

make our names sound like
sacrifice, like falling through black
holes and being pulled apart
without knowing it

Every time someone says
do you remember ____
we say we don't, we never count
the ones of us who no longer
are our own

we never liked to lose,
but sometimes we practice
remembering what they looked
like: her eyes, her nose, the way
she moved

and if no one is watching us
we might even
whisper how much
we miss her hair,
tangling in our fingers

as she made some joke
about someone we all despised

All Melusine's Daughters

Our skin itches just below the
surface, a tickle in the throat of
our veins.

This feeling of hands on our
skin, stroking our thighs
and inching down our bellies.

In stories from centuries ago,
our skin was cursed,
befouled by Gods or just because

in these stories, we cursed our bodies
and the weight of our skin
as it changed us, shaped us, made us.

We wanted out, out, out and we'd arch
our backs, scream out to the Gods to free us from our skin

but these are stories, and now we only
arch our backs, scream
names in pleasure, from hands upon our skin

can we dig our nails so
deep that our skin
comes undone?

It seemed so simple, if
our skin could slip off,
watching snakes push their way out.

Our new skin is so smooth,
the surface shiny as the blood in our
veins.

The Detective, Years After

Missing women often appear
to me in dreams, always asking

the same questions: why it was her that I
had found instead of them,
why she was the one brought home

alive, fighting the twisting, a
rush that crept up through her
body.

Years later, she would say to me: *Most
days, I think I will start screaming and never
stop.*

The wind will sometimes wake me from
dreams, inciting the trees outside to tap
codes onto my windows,
Morse message pleas for me to stir,

and the women will be waiting at
the foot of the bed or standing by
the window or leaning over me to
whisper secrets in my ears— locations of their bodies,

the depth of dirt that presses down on them, the
feel of decomposition
—and I never know how to
tell them I am sorry I
stopped looking.

The missing women ask me why I never found
them; I try to answer
but words come out

sounding only like the crush of dead leaves under
foot as I searched.

A Breath Expelled

I never told you that I spend my nights chasing demons
because I thought you'd say that was passé, that demon-
chasing was for teenage girls or men with too much time on
their hands
And the demons I know are the ones with bad credit
and they're easy to find, they hang out in the downtown diner
where you can get midnight stacks of pancakes slathered in
too much butter for less than two dollars

The first demon I saw was when I was in college and someone
bent my fingers back until they snapped but when I tell
people this they only ever say "oh that explains why your
pinky is so crooked."
So I never told you that sometimes I even chase them in my
sleep
because I thought that you'd say that I needed to let go, that
dreams of demons were holding me back

And the demons I dream are the ones with low voices
who wear tight jeans and lean over me in cafes to ask what
I'm reading and, you know, in dreams I'm always reading the
same stupid book

The first demon I tracked was the one who kept the names of
the dead tattooed on his skin and he liked to go shirtless, show
off how the names moved, how they wept when the sun hit
them

But I never told you that I know my demons because I
thought you'd find that strange, that I would keep them
curled in my mind, a sense memory of what not to do

And the demons I know are the ones I can deal with
because they're easy to spot, with their shining eyes
and their fingers always just slightly too thin

The first demon I met was just like them all and now I know what to look for, know to let you speak first and I will cast them from your body if you let me

Once They Sainted a Mermaid

It is always the same stories that we tell of
women with fish tails and hair caught full of
seaweed and we never remember how the feel of
water constant and pressing must have been. She
saw villages overtaken by waves, she imagined
constellations of star fish, and when she wept it
tasted the same as the sea and so she never knew
when she was actually sad. Her fingers caressed
the bones of sailors, drowned in storm or mutiny,
and she thought that men were only skeletons,
and she wondered how they danced, if they
clicked and clattered as they did. She fell in love
with a shark once, but the shark left her behind,
movement was life, forward was breath. She
spent one morning watching the sky filter down
to her and then she was given the choice between
eternity under and a moment with the sun. And
in the flash of dissolving, of filled with stars, of
glow, she thought she remembered land, how it
was to feel the earth turning beneath her feet, like
dancing.

Flight

I don't give in to much
not the palm reader
who tells me that hope is something
good, not the scratch tickets
kept under glass with all that
empty promise waiting, not even
your voice on the other end
of the phone sounding
like you mean what you're saying.

When I find a field of dandelions,
wispy heads held high, my nephews
pull me to it. They grab handfuls
for making as many wishes
as they can. I know that this
is folktale, is dandelion propaganda
at its best—make a wish, spread
the seeds into the air. I know this
as well as I know that some things
never work out, that some people's
lives never quite match up, that
there is only so much we can do
so much of the time.

Still here is the thing: My nephews
were laughing, making wishes, blowing
dandelion fuzz at one another, seeds
filling the air like adventurers going
off in search of some place fortunate,
and one nephew passes me a stem.
Up close, the tops of dandelions
look like alien planets in movies on TV
late at night. So strange, so easy to
let go of. My nephew says "make a wish"
and so, just once, I do.

Exposing Tricks

My body is ready
still on hard table, arms to sides
my body is ready

Things I have learned to do: slip my hands from cuffs as easily
as I can slip out of my clothes, shed the metal to floor

The Davenport Brothers were famous for
spirit cabinets, for locking the dead into
place and hearing them moan.

I have pressed my hands to walls, have felt your body against
mine, have listened to the sound of your heart beating fast and
hard

My body is ready
waiting for you, for swords
my body is ready

Things I have learned to do: not flinch when knives sink into
wall around me, skimming past me so narrowly that they pin
my clothes, not flinch when imagining all those almost cuts on
my skin

Others exposed the Davenport
Brothers, lit flames in
the dark, revealing the tangle
of limbs moving.

My body is ready
breath fast, heart pounding
my body is ready

Things I have learned to do: open my mouth wide, feel your
fingertips caress my lips, as you pull roses from my throat,
careful the thorns don't cut my tongue

Still there were so many
who came back again
and again, willing to be
fooled, to see the dead
live.

My body is ready
skin hot, breath fast
my body is ready

Things I have learned to do: stay so still as to seem dead,
holding breath as I count the alphabet up and count it again,
so still that the audience gasps, leans forward, begs you to
wake me

Others say the trickery involved
was an innocent kind-
ness, letting hope fill the
audiences, breath into bodies.

My body is ready
holding breath, waiting
my body is ready to let you in

I was Planning on Learning to Breathe Today

The best way to practice
swimming is to learn
how to drown.

I have tried this for so long:
throw myself into what
I'm afraid will happen,
get used to it before
it can.

When I was a child, I practiced
holding my breath:
in bathtubs, in troughs of
icy water, in lakes,

I held it so long I saw spots,
imagined shapes underwater.

I wanted to be Houdini, be
someone who escaped
death over and over.

I can still drink a large bottle
of water without taking a break
I still love that first breath
afterwards.

Someone told me once
the best way to save yourself
when drowning is to give in.
don't panic,

often giving in feels the same
as escape
at first

often escape feels
like breathing.

Twisting the Aces

"In magic today, as always, the effect is what counts."
—Dai Vernon

Apocalypse Scenario

In the event of a zombie apocalypse, living
in the city will most likely mean
your death. Infection spreads fast
when our bodies are close
together. The CDC releases

preparation for what they deem
impossible, because it's good
to know about infection
and they want people to actually read it.

Zombies are more palatable
than thinking about the diseases
we should see coming: the influenzas,

the viruses, the things our mothers
warned us about. Wash your hands,
cover your mouth, protect

yourself. There are so many things
more likely to kill us
than zombies, like waiting too long

to go to the doctor, like the slippery tub,
like being in a crowded place,

like not smiling
at the wrong man, like saying
no, like trying so hard

to believe that everything
will be alright. In the event
of a zombie apocalypse,
rural areas will have some time

to prepare. Still, in the event,
it is best to run, to go to
empty places, to try not

to remember

the feel of bodies pressing
close to you in crowds.

You'd Be Home Now

They're putting a mobile network on the moon
and I joke, "I want to sext it"
but it's not such a joke really
how I would like to seduce
the infinite, use my tongue
to collapse galaxies in on themselves
over and over, let the stars find new
ways to make my body ache
in such relief
there has always been something
between lost
and saved about the way I feel
thinking about space.
I wanted to tell you that once
but didn't know how to explain
there is a rush
in distance
in the long pull between
bodies who have found
one another but haven't yet
touched
the ecliptic orbit
of planets, the spin
away from and towards
is a slow building
catastrophe to a crashing
release.
There has always been something
between distance
and belonging about the way I feel
thinking about space
and I wonder if you've ever
felt that too.
There is a danger in this,
the inevitability of destruction
but I would let my body be
undone by the weight
of galaxies, the way

that space would unfold
around me, I would
say the names of a thousand
stars, finding
every point of pleasure
on this celestial map
until we got lost into
one another.
There has always been something
between finding
and wanting about the way I feel
thinking about space
the closest I get to knowing
what it might be
 is when I think
about you.

Error Coding

301 Moved Permanently
Your body is still an arc, a part of this curve we called our
own. I miss you most in the memory of your walk, or the way
you stretched your calf muscles out by balancing on different
points of your feet, or the scar across the back of your hand,
the white, ridged skin-tattoo you never chose.

502 Bad Gateway
Remember that house we looked at in a city we visited?   It
was open and the realtor led us through with a smile. You
whispered, "Imagine who we'd be if we lived here." And I
said, "If we lived here, we'd be home now." But maybe you'd
never seen those ads, because you only replied, "Yes."

530 Site is Frozen
Winter came early, and you watched your breath leave your
mouth,
wondered if there was a word for people who read fortunes in
the shapes made by breath. You said it was so cold you could
taste it.
"What does it remind you of?" You ordered me to tell you.

451 Redirect
The wine was the color of a bad bruise. It seemed like it only
existed to stain: lips, furniture, the white dress I wore because
I'm an idiot. You spent the night talking to everyone else and
I didn't know anyone so I stood in corners and tried to smile.

444 No Response
The phone rings in the other room. In the car, music on, that
one song we listened to over and over. Knocking on the door.

100 Continue
Later, I will think of the conversations we started. The ones
interrupted. When you were explaining something to me. Or I
was telling you about the dream I had. Something always
came up. There is just this now: the unfinished.

300 Multiple Choices

In the dream I never finished telling, I was taking a test in a classroom without windows. My childhood best friend stood in front of the room, playing with a slinky. She said, "Jesus Christ, have you ever tried to make these things go backwards?" And I broke down crying, unable to keep filling out the bubbles on my scantron. I wasn't sad or frustrated or angry and the tears tasted like rainbow sherbet.

103 Checkpoint

Your hands. Your mouth. The weight of your body. These specifics that add up to a person are what we dwell on after the loss. That the lips on mine will never again be your lips, your hands on my skin, the press of a body into mine will never again be yours.

520 Unknown Error

We can trace everything to its roots. It's what we are especially good at. Yet still we cannot find any explanation there.

But Also This Is Why the Robots Always Turn On Us

It is not the moment when they first
open their eyes and suddenly see
the world as it is.

It is not when they learn to move their
bodies with one another, to find
pleasure in the workings of machines.

It is not after they watch destruction
on live stream videos from around
the world, not even when the images

plague their sleep. And, no, it is not even
when they first begin to dream,
to find patterns in the night sky, or

does the pattern repeat, is it a simulation of
a dream, a glitch? And, yet, it is still
not when they begin to think of questions

before answers when before there were only

solutions. It is instead when you caress the
bones that have never been born, place
them together and try to think of names

you can give to those you plan to never hold
in your arms.

For Someone Who Doesn't Have to Believe in Monsters

I play my cards so close to my chest
they might as well be tattoos.
When people ask me for my past
I tell them the things that chase away
the truth—the secret to not lying
is to never get close to needing to so
I say I'm scared of horses
and silverfish and leopard seals.
I distract with the things they'll find
funny or if they ask what I want to do
with my life and I change the subject
say some random fact from history:
that Edgar Allan Poe may have died
from rabies, that there were ships
in WWI called "razzle dazzles," that onions
make you cry because sulphenic
acids are unstable and can rearrange into
gases, that each of a person's eyes has a blindspot
that is never noticed because the eyes work together
to correct the gap.
But here's the thing, if you were the one who asked me
for some truth
I'd tell you my life, unravel it between us
so that you could see it from above, every
secret I'd give you, until you held them all
in your hands because
I think you might tell me
what I'm not seeing.

My Mother Always Told Me We Lived in Haunted Times

Old bits of farm machinery
scatter across our property
in acres long since gone wild—
grape vines curled amorous
around rust-stolen wheels,

pitchfork tines hit by our
glistening shovel heads as we
dig for diggings sake,

the pleasant push and toss,

the smell of old metal,
distinct and crisp like a
lake in autumn, when the
algae turns from
emerald to copper.

This hasn't been a farm for
almost a century—these are
spirits we imagine we keep
finding: sharp, and ancient,
and almost like bones.

Sci-Fi Lesson

In the movie *The Thing*, no one
makes it out

we don't know that for sure
but we can feel it.

How do you come back
from that kind of knowing?

That everyone you know can
be someone you don't know

underneath their skin. The blood
is what gives them away,

shies from the heat,
but we can't all bleed

to find out if we are
who we thought we were.

Quick-change

"Look at this life—all mystery and magic."
                —Harry Houdini

Sleepwalking

Don't wake him, that's the first thing you think when you
find your sleeping lover walking through the house at night.

Remember your cousin, when you were eight or nine, who told
you about a boy who was woken while sleepwalking, and the
shock killed him. Dead, right there, boom, your cousin said,
smacking her hands together.

Your lover washes his hands at the sink, eyes closed, and you
wonder what he is dreaming about: cooking?

Remember the time you dreamed about standing in a kitchen
at night and your great grandmother, years in the grave, sat
at the table, asking you to make potato pancakes with sour
cream and chives.

But, you only had a fridge filled with asparagus and lemons.
In dreams you should, at least, be able to please the dead.
And sitting down beside your great grandmother you began to
weep, and she cradles you in her arms.
The tears sustenance enough.

Your lover walks to the window, still sleeping, and presses his
forehead to the glass. You wonder if the cold would wake him.
Then, you notice he is crying. Tears from out of his closed
eyes.

What dreams do we dream, you wonder, when we think we are
unwatched? You want to hold him, lead him back to bed, but
don't wake him, you think. Let him sleep.

Abandoned Houses

You ask forgiveness before
you've done anything wrong
you say one day you will

let me down
like a promise, like when you tell
me your past in flickers
how much of you I need

to fill in myself
your secrets less secrets
than hungered for spaces

I cant imagine myself
inside of
like houses on Halloween

who keep their doors closed
but the thing is: as a child,
those were the houses

I understood the most,
knowing how much they'd
miss, all those tricks

treats, all those ways
I might ask them
for something

they could never give.

A Reward For You and The Ones I Don't Think You Need

After the rush
      of our bodies aligned
            you told me the true story of the time you
found a woman
buried beneath the tree outside your family's home
      you were seven and your tiny shovel
            hit what you knew would be treasure
but unearthed the smooth white of skull
      with teeth so perfect and even
            that you imagined that smile for years

The police came with tape and tools
      and cordoned off the tree you loved to climb
            they unburied the woman bone
by bone until each piece of her shone
      under moonlight and you thought she just
            might reform into something almost
living some skeleton who could go home to her
      family and make them meals she couldn't eat
            could find a job as a dentist's model

But the police just took the bones away
      and your parents asked no questions
            and you never found out her name
and didn't you ever look her up
      I asked incredulous as I lay
            in your arms our limbs
still entwined our sweat now mixed
      the taste of you on my lips
            and you shrugged

In your dreams sometimes you said
      you imagine the life she lived
            before she became the scary
story told in your neighborhood for years
      passed from children like unwanted
            flavors of gummy bears
and the life you imagined her was something

        good and bright and her death so accidental
           that you never wanted to prove

yourself wrong.

Questions for Men Falling Through Space

When you were a child did you dream of the stars? Were they so bright, you woke up momentarily blinded?

> Like that time you walked too far out into the snow drowned field and everything around you was white, white, white.

Or did this love come later? A reaching to grasp galaxies. You told someone you loved once that her eyes reminded you of the night sky but she wasn't sure what you meant. You weren't sure what you meant. Are you sure now?

Is there someone who loves you enough to have let you go easily? Is there someone who you will think about as the darkness breaks up the light around you? Will you think about the way it felt

> when you found a rhythm in their body, felt the heat of their skin on yours, and they said your name over and over and over.

Did you tell anyone about the nightmare you had where you walked out into a field, towards a dying tree in the center, and the closer you got the more you heard someone calling your name? Is that what this reminds you of most? Are you scared?

Does time stop? Does sound stop? Does everything just stop?

> A memory of your mother cooking, stirring something on the stove, and she turns to you and says
> "I thought you were your father for a second."

Do you regret this pursuit of the sky? Are the stars so hungry they can hardly wait to taste you? Do you wish you'd stayed with feet on Earth?

Is there someone you've left behind who will wake up and know somehow that you are gone? What would you want to tell them?

Would you say: I'm sorry? Would you say: I love you? Would you say: I'll miss you? Would you say that it's like:

> The time you were sledding with your brother, down a hill that you shouldn't have been on. It was so tall and steep and the sled went so fast and you thought that this was a mistake, that you both would get hurt, would die, and then you slowed to a stop and found yourself still alive, still fine, and laughing you climbed back to the top.

Is it exactly like that?

The Witch's House

There are dishes in the sink again
        piled like teetering Jenga blocks
                when they crash, there will be something close
                    to exclamation.

My mother told me: be kind, be good, be caring
My mother told me: trust people until give you a reason not to
My mother told me: revenge is a dish best served on sparkling
clean plates

He spends most nights away from home,
and I like to fall asleep to silence,
to the sound of no one in this house but myself
        Someone told me once that I slept like I was lost in
        space, arms flung out to catch the debris from dying
        stars,
        and I think they meant it as an insult,
        or a you-need-to-take-up-less-room,
        but I heard it as the highest compliment
        because I've always wanted to spend
        my nights arcing past planets,
        tasting the solar system

There are books on the table
        pens, pads of paper, dice from some game
                and none of it is mine. Am I the only one
                    who has been told to not take up
    space?

My mother told me: be kind, be good, be trustworthy
My mother told me: believe in other people until they let you
down
My mother told me: the most important part of war is to kill
your enemy with kindness

He leaves his dishes in the sink, his life cast out over the table,
says he likes ants as they crawl over the sink
        A book I read once said that a homemade remedy

for ants is to clean with vinegar, the
smell of it keeps them from being able to find their
way home through scent and they get
lost and frightened and try to remember if they've
ever been loved at all.

There are spells I've been taught
        things to incant, objects to place in bowls:
                a bit of paper with writing on it, half-eaten
apple,
                        or some dice maybe once played with.

My mother told me: be kind, be good, be true
My mother told me: forgive other people, until they go too far
My mother told me: use this power only when you must

Insert Bad Joke Here

Make it a pun or make it something only we get—a reference
to the time the restaurant served water flecked with crystals
of salt because it wanted to give the feeling of the ocean,
though we were in the Midwest and outside puddles of gray
slush dappled the sidewalks.

We laughed about that for days, until tears streamed down
our face and into our mouths and the salt-salt of it made us
howl even more.

Make it the kind of joke you only find on popsicle sticks. The
kind about monsters—what's the title of the werewolf's
famous poem?
"Howl." I remember the sound of your laugh sometimes so
clearly that it makes my skull ache with the vibration of it. Is
this

a kind of phantom pain? What's that joke you told me about
the ghost who reviewed movies? Sometimes, though less now,
I think of you and can't get a breath. My throat tightens,
chest aches, skin feels briefly on fire. I smell dirty snow
melting, hear the sound of seagulls where they should never
be, I over-react to things no one else notices. Oh, here, the end
of the joke. The ghost was fired

because he found every film haunting.

This Has All Happened Before

The radio keeps cutting out
        and on the other end of the phone
                you are telling me something important. So
loud.

It sounds like "Don't listen to the dead, they speak
        in sestinas." On the radio, Sam Cooke sings
                you thrill me, honest you do. So low.

It's not raining but almost, the air
        heavy with water and the road
                ahead glistens. My mother would say drive
slow.

Last year, around this time, we spent
        so many hours under the covers,
                finding ways to make the other gasp. Fast and
slow, slow.

I am losing you, the signal growing weaker
        around these curves, near these trees.
                You tell me you feel "so a—" What? Alone?

The dead are speaking, a woman said to me,
        at a carnival, when I was the height of
                my mother's waist. Hear it in your soul.

I'll call you back when I'm off the road, out
        of the forest, I'll call you back.
                Sam sings *but it's lasted so long.*

I'm Glad You Won't Be Able to Find Something I Think You Could

There's a car in the parking lot that only
drives in at midnight,

its engine like the mating-call growl
of some beast that is the last of its kind,
an endling of menace.

You always sleep through the things
that scare me the most,
your body so still and breath so even
that I wonder if you're playing.

Once, I ran my hand across your chest
and whispered the things I wanted
you to do to me to see if you'd stir
but you've always been better
at these games than me.

I always try to find my peace
in you, body tucked close,
your breath on my skin
as you talk,

your dreaming voice
like the version of you I never
met, someone who might not want me.

The car revs, you don't stir.
I keep my eyes on the ceiling

but it's too dark to see.

What the Earth Returns to Our Mouths

We have eaten dirt, still clinging
to the beets we thought we washed

clean, so careful, so impossible to get every bit

                    and there is nothing we can do for
                    you, say the birds, pecking at our skin

                    they think we taste as sweet as candy
                    canes, as overripe pawpaw fruit.

We have been eating so much earth, it sticks between our
teeth

rich and dark and even our
hair grows silky with the clay

                    and there is nothing we will do for
                    you, say the roots of trees, pushing

                    through our bones, up and up,
                    as if our ribs are ladders.

We try to remember to clean,
clean the skin, until it bleeds

red into the lines of our hands,
this color, it looks so familiar.

Little Skin Teeth

On Wednesday, I find my teeth
sharpened while I slept.
It's a strange thing to get used to:
I can't stop running

my tongue over the points.

My lover gets nervous, says,
"Whoa, whoa, you know
this could make some things
really difficult."
He looks scared

but he feeds me fruit
in bed, tenderly for breakfast—my fangs
press into pawpaw
flesh, custard sweet

and delicate. That night, my lover sleeps
with back turned, bodies at rest
look as inviting as the sea.

My skin is toughening, I can feel it
embracing me.

I've heard that shark skin
is like this: strong,
"dermal denticles"

On Thursday morning, my love
peels back the blankets to study
my body in the half
light of morning.

He says "look at my teeth" and
his fangs are like slivers of light
drawing the dark
from the room—

I wonder if we will swim

through the air, if we will have to keep going forward
or if we will be allowed this
moment—

silent in our bedroom
as we learn how to adjust to a new evolution.

We Who Vanish

I say to him that Jean Robert-Houdin once made a tree
blossom into life. Houdini took his name from him. And
Steven
Millhauser used that trick for his Eisenheim. And I'm thinking
about how that tree must have felt springing upwards as the
wind-up butterfly swam circles through the air.

He changes the subject, says he dreamed my feet were
bleeding. I've been doing a lot of walking. The soles of my
shoes are worn almost smooth, and so my footprints seem
blank. Sometimes I walk to the café to order hot chocolate
with shots of espresso, and I try to sit and just sit but my feet
keep tapping the floor. I've seen tigers pace cages at zoos and
I wonder if this is why—their bodies still hold the memory of
the walking they've done, and it courses through their blood
like some impossible musical beat that they can never quite
catch up to.

He tells me I'm doing it again, like when he asked me about
my religion as if it was something as concrete as mathematics:
addition, subtraction, a Fibonacci sequence of devotion. I said
that poets have found death in a handful of dust or seen hell
collapse behind them step by step. They do not tell me of
heaven because there is no space for it. I said that there are
prayers even to say upon witnessing lightning. That flash of
light burned imprints on my eyes, and for days I saw it and
thought I was witnessing the divine. I once was blinded by the
sun reflected on a lake. I once was lost. But now I'm—I said
that I don't always trust my image in mirrors. I said I've
never
been in love but I've fallen for love. I've counted up beads and
thrown salt over my shoulders and held my breath when
passing graveyards. I said that I've touched
light bulbs still hot, and it felt just the same as
trying to explain.

He sighs and says, go back to magic, and so I do, I think
that if I had been there then, some audience member

in from the cold, I would
have watched with breath held. And when that tree

unfurled and the butterfly danced out to us,
well I think right then I might have believed
in anything.

He Was Always Almost Something

Sometimes he'd write words on
blackboards solely because he
liked the way chalk dust
softened his fingertips, paled
them into a color not quite
living.

Once he ate earth
accidentally
it tasted bitter rich like
dark chocolate drenched in
coffee grounds or ash.

He never drank flames, though
he meant to, after a childhood
night at the circus when he
watched a fire-eater delight the
crowd by never dying a single
time.

When Everyone Else Says After

The phone rings, trilling
field of crickets, and

She still runs to pick
it up, breathless "hello"

And it's never for her, anymore,
and she holds it out

to her mother, father,
sister, or hangs up "wrong number"

At night she dreams deep of
her best friend, sitting

on a stone-strewn lake
shore. She is gathering

Pebbles, piling them up
on her lap, glistening

Against her dark-washed
jeans. Her best friend

Picks up one, small and round
and white as snow cones before

The syrup drench, and she
places it in her mouth. She

Swallows it, one gulp, and
says it's for "safe-keeping."

Long in the Tooth

Upon discovering
that it actually only meant that
the gums recede with age
I was disappointed,
a little, that
it wasn't about how
teeth might have kept
       growing imperceptibly
until Grandmother could look
up at the wolf and
declare,
in mild wonder,
"My what
       big teeth we have."

Osteomancy

Have you found my bones yet?
I left them in odd
corners of your apartment—
tucked at the base of the too
small tub (where we tried once to
slip under the water together
but our knees knocked awkwardly
and we both laughed, you brushed
my hair from my face with soapy
hand and I wanted you then
even covered in foam), slipped
into the back of your closet (you
kept your shirts hung up but
never ordered by color, I kept myself
from rearranging them), even
under your pillow (you always curled
one arm under and the other arm
over, as if you were fighting to keep
your pillow in place, as if it might
run away from you in your dreams).
I wonder if you will recognize them,
so clean and brittle away from me, if
you will remember what it felt like
to move your body with mine, the times
you'd bend my knees or I'd arc my spine
to fit the press of you. Will you be
cleaning and pick one up, trace its shape
with your fingers, place it in your mouth,
let your tongue slide over the smooth, trying
to taste it. Will you keep it
warm in the heat
of your mouth?
Because that's what I do with yours.

Just Kidding, I Already Did

Sometimes I think I'll remember
the things from the list
I keep in my pocket or
on the fridge or even once
written on the palm of my hand.

It's easy enough to teach
yourself ways of keeping
track: mnemonics and palaces
and I Love You
means Ice Lettuce Yogurt.

But it's harder to know
that you really remember—
that the city smelled like lilacs
and rising bread, that
the river was colored like
amber, or was it cola?

Is cola something you want
to remember as beautiful or
should it be prettier when
you try to draw it back to you?

I dream so much
of things I've lost
that they feel like stories,
like never was.

Sometimes I think I'll try
to remember you, if we
ever lose one another, and
you'll just be almost,
be just this side of
nearly there.

So I'll write you down
in lists, I'll keep

you in my pocket, on
the palm of my hand,
I'll try so hard

that you'll be here.

Hidden in Question is that We Must Go on a Journey

The point, you told me,
is the question
        not the answer
but I wasn't listening,
too busy hanging over
the side of the bed
to see if I could get
that tingling feeling
in my head
        and you put your hand
        on my stomach to get
                my attention
        but I was seeing stars
        and your hand was warm
        as cups of tea
        and sometimes all I want
        is for you to keep touching
        my skin
                but you got distracted
                by some thought that
                        wasn't me
                and took your hand
                away, started talking
                about the structure
                of arguments
                and I let the spinning
                room call me to sleep.

Cooking with Turmeric

We do not mean to stain
our skin, only later
notice the golden hues
to our fingertips, palms

as we rinse our hands
under ice water, and you
lean into me, saying, "we're
glowing"

In years, I will have
forgotten
even the precise way you
spoke—each word always
so perfectly enunciated, but

I will remember this
moment clearly, how
the kitchen lights glint
off our skin and the lines
of our palms stand out
so distinctly.

The stains
wash away eventually,
but for awhile, our hands
hold
such clear fortunes.

Kitchen Piece

For breakfast, we had the most amazing French toast with
lemon curd, and there could be a story there. In the way that
French toast dates back to the Roman Empire—to gladiators
and emperors but that in France, they call it
'pain perdu' or lost bread. Designed to bring it back to
edibility, to flavor, to something we crave on mornings when
the clouds cover the sun and the air holds itself closed and
gray. Or maybe the story

is about lemons, how they glint like gold in hot groves, how
the lemon tree in our greenhouse can never bear fruit, only
bursting with flowers such heavy sweet scent, or even how the
lemon is a cross between bitter
oranges and citrons. But really, we do

not need to seek out stories in places other than the thick
bread dipped in egg, dash of cinnamon, vanilla, nutmeg,
sizzling in pan. The way you stirred the lemon curd, wrist so
practiced, so confident, and
I licked the sour from spoon, waiting

for the first bite. For the taste, for you to sit down, tell me
something of the dream you had last night. There is enough of
this to feed us for a thousand days.

Conjuring Orange Trees

"The average man is not hard to mystify"
—Howard Thurston

Lichenometry

A friend adds me to a Facebook group where people post
pictures of mushrooms, mosses, lichen
such tender stalks fill my screen between
the statuses of friends whose voices
I no longer remember.

There are so many types
of mosses, they flood
the page with colors
I can't touch.

Sometimes this makes me think
of you, the miles between us
that stretch empty between
my hands and your skin
your hands and my skin.

You told me once that lichen
exists everywhere. Something
like six percent of the world
is covered in it, this symbiotic

relationship stretches and
stretches. Or maybe I just
hear it in your voice because
it seems like something you'd tell
me, one of those small facts

you give to me
until I dream in them.

If I could tell you where
we'd be in five years, ten,
I think I wouldn't

I think I'd instead share
some photo with you
of some mushroom

growing in
an unfamiliar place.

The Current Will Push and Pull You

My boyfriend studies jellyfish
he says they could hold
so many secrets

In bed, when he's kissing
the hollow of my throat,
the crook of my elbow,
he sometimes tells me

scientific facts
like they are I Love Yous
like how few jellies
can actually stay together

that's why it's a bloom, not
really a swarm, he says
but I don't get the difference.

Sometimes when our bodies
are still pressed together,
as we wait for our heart beats
to slow together,

he tells me about all ways
in which the world
has changed the ocean

he tells me how blooms
are becoming more frequent
how the water has lost so

much and the jellyfish
are filling in the darkness.

Here's something I learned
that he never told me:
jellyfish reproduce

without ever really touching
I wanted to tell him

one night
when our bodies were
still entangled together

but I thought he must
have already known.

Plantings

A rareish fruit,
the heartbeat
we grow it from our fingertips
from you holding me

asking if it's okay
if we can stay this close

its roots get tangled
in our throats
in the press of our bodies

we feed it with time
and distance and never
saying what we want

sometimes they ripen
too quick
rot into sour, into
voices caught on empty

or they ripen
too slow, forget
to be eaten up
never held in our mouths

we grow it from our fingertips
from you holding me

we break through the peel
juice on our tongues
holding the seeds
in our hands

until we can hear them
through our skin.

Cephalofoil

The eye doctor gives me a look
of concern when he asks,
"do you drive?"
I say no, I have never—
and he says, "well, that's good.
You have barely any peripheral
vision. Have you ever noticed that?"

Have I ever noticed the things
I don't notice? I shake my head,
although it explains
so much.

As a child, I loved hammerhead
sharks, the shape of them,
the way they never looked ahead
and so could not see
the future.

Later, I learned researchers believe
the sharks evolved that way
to see above and below them
to see more than we can
imagine.

Knowledge too is a kind
of loss,

but no one has ever died
from a hammerhead shark
and they are still
almost extinct.

"I bet you're easy to surprise"
the eye doctor jokes,
and I nod,
because I'm always
failing to notice

what to look out for.

& Other Ways to Read the Dirt

What have we done to one another?
What grievances have we let seep
into the soil, we dig our fingers
into the ground as if we wish to
tear out our

own hair by the roots. You know,
we have filled the trees with
oranges like poison, remember
that tree at the beginning of time
and the serpent and the apple

and what poison did we taste then
upon our tongues, was knowledge
about what we could do in war?

Was war what we learned, or was it
always in us, rotting us up from
the ground as we stumbled away
from cities burning, from villages
sprayed with chemicals, from the sight

of the world undone by us. We pray
sometimes for a god, any, to hear us
and forgive us, and cleanse us of our sins.
Our sins, so filled with colors,
etched across the skin of
the land.

We Imagined Their Fossils to be Thunderbolts

I have never wanted
children
never been the kind
to dream of daughters
or give those imagined futures
such pretty names.

You're good with kids
someone tells me
and it's not untrue

I can love what
I don't want, can tell
my nephews stories
about magic and spiders

and trees whose roots
crack down through
history and even sometimes
into other lives.

Here's a memory I have
of being a child:
in the ocean, I stepped
on a sea urchin

a sharp spine
stabbed into the arch
of my foot
blood welled

when I pulled it
free. I worried
for years, worry still

what harm I must
have done

If You Lived Here

Walking home, I took a path
I hadn't used in weeks
and where a month ago
there was a line of houses,
one family homes,
there was now just mud,
an excision of someone
else's memories.

I turned around once, circling
myself to belief, thinking I
was somehow lost, had taken
a turn wrong. But my city
is small and every path
leads me home eventually.

The mud smelled empty,
cleaned out of earth, not
the clay rich dense of
where I once grew up.

There's a house on the land
where my family lives
that hasn't held people
in decades but I used
to have dreams most
nights that it did

It seemed so strange
every time I went
there during the day,
to find it empty,
as if I had stepped
into its future

There is a strangeness
to houses emptied
of their people

an emptiness
to land estranged
from its houses

Lacunae

My nephew calls me up
on the phone, often, just
so he can hang up on me.

There is joy in loss when
we are small

that someone can be there
and then gone

mothers playing peek-a-boo and
we can't help the glee escaping
our mouths in giggles.

Once, a friend and I were driving
on a road she knew well from
childhood

when she pulled in her breath
a sharp inhale of ache

and she stopped the car, pulled
to the side of the road
and stared at an empty field

"What's wrong?" I asked and
she pointed at the field,
the bits of grass,

"There used to be a house here.
It's like it never existed."

And together we stared at the blankness
that before I thought was something full.

Duolingo

I am learning to speak
another tongue again:
rolling my r's and clicking
tip to roof of mouth. The first
things we learn are the I ams
and I dos.

We learn I like you
much earlier than I love you,
they are not either harder
than the other but maybe the extra
time is to prepare us.
We learn quickly: thank you,
my name is, I can speak, I need,
I want, I can't.

We learn in sets, in ways of
conjugation, can find a map
beneath the speaking.
I meant to tell you once
that I liked your laugh,
but I held my tongue.

There are so many languages I could
say I love you in and don't.
The first phrase I learn
in any language always is:
I'm sorry.

Thread the Water

Someone told me once that squid
are mostly alone,
that when photographed,

there is almost always
only one flitting
past the camera, past

the divers, past whoever
is looking.

Giant squids aren't
as strong as they look,
their strength not

in proportion to their size.
Their dead though,
washing up on shores,

created so many myths
of how they could terrorize,
how they could break

ships apart with their tentacles.
We make such myths

of our monsters
on a video
a squid slips

past the screen
into the dark
beyond our sight.

In time, another
will flicker across
the footage and

I wonder will the two
ever meet?

There is No Matter

We find our necessity
in vacuums:

of space, of sound, of time, of
the whoosh-whooshing of
your grandmother swishing
through the rooms of her
mostly empty home.

You have a new friend
who tells you: I wish you
knew me when I was
happy, I liked me better
then. She sucks iced tea
through a neon straw and
it sounds like drains, like
feet getting stuck in the
just-rained-on mud.

Your grandmother told you, once,
that cleaning is the best way to
remember you're alive: the traces
through dust, the evapor-
ating smear of soap on glass.

Your friend calls you to say:
she can't hear your voice through
the line. You sound like you've
been pulled through tunnels, she says.

Once, you were young enough to
sit cross-legged on chairs, as
your grandmother swooped
around you. She said: I wish
I was born now, so I could grow up to
be an astronaut.

The mouth of the Hoover drank dust

from under your chair.
Your grandmother said:
space must strip so
much away when it
holds you.

Other Words for Wanting

I held spring under my tongue for a week kept close as secrets

like your name, like the color of your eyes when you are not
you in my dreams

Mud grabs my boots, holding me still for a second longer
than I'm meant to be kept

like you in the morning, with one arm across me, pretending
to sleep still as if that alone will hold me

Geese come back and hover over ice-licked ponds that haven't
yet decided what form they want
to keep—to hold or to give in

like what I've wondered about when thinking what to tell
you— here I am or you found me or I am yours

Spring comes close enough for the wind to smell as rich as
earth uncovered and held, I try
to keep it in my lungs

like the idea of you makes me try sometimes to not smile
when I see you across a room

I keep my face still, my gaze steady, until you are close
enough
to hold

Other Heights

You know those climbers on Everest?
The ones who never came down.
I hear that they're still intact—perfect sculptures of who they
once were.
Some fairy tale logic, but would a kiss be warm enough to
melt their lips?
And what would you do in the world where it was?
Where all our dead could be returned to us so easily.
I heard they were found by a man who didn't plan on reaching
the top.
His summit was them.
How did they look to him?
Were they statues or ghosts or just men asleep?
He must have stared for a while, blinking to make sure it
wasn't a trick.
Some act of snow blindness.
Did he think for a second about how strange it was?
Or remember the stories like this?
The ones Medusa changed to stone, the woman becoming
salt for one last look, that treacherous
mountain to the water of life and those pebbles
are the souls of men and so much
prettier than bones.
When he reached out for them was it in surprise?
Or was it in elation that someone had finally found them?
These young men come to ice.

Grow Your Own Little Forest

1.

We give our pasts to trees
there are so many stories
about how the roots hold
our world, hold our truths.

I told someone once I could never love
a man who couldn't love
a forest, couldn't find the spaces where
the world is digging itself
into memory.

My earliest memories are of limbs,
of resting my tiny body against
tree trunks, of the smell of the earth
when I pressed my hands into it—
what futures can be read
in the way dirt clings to our palm lines?

2.

There are trees we point out
because they have survived,
finding hope in the years
contained in them

a friend once showed me a tree
trunk, pointed out where there
had been rough years, "look,"
he said, "you can see when
it was hurt."

The human body can be like
that too. We find the losses
only when viewed after the fact.

3.

On the campus where I work,
the tops of trees are dying, shedding
bark and going white as bones,
the limbs stretched up
like skeleton hands
and my brother tells me
to bring him a sample,
says there might be something
that can be fixed.

In Sweden, there's a tree
whose roots have grown
for over 9,000 years.
Imagine the objects they
have reached past,
the lives who have lived
above them, told secrets
held hands
kissed
and given up
on one another
as the roots keep pushing.

On my parents' land
there's a willow tree
that survived a tornado,
a lightning strike,
so many years of breaking,
before it finally fell down.
And still cuttings from it
could be regrown, rerooted.

4.

I saw a story the other day
about a tree in Georgia

that owns itself, so that
no one can cut it down,
can claim the land at its base.

In myths, there are so many
trees who were once people
and I wonder what their loved
ones thought—did they visit
those limbs? Wrap arms
around them? Did they still
tell them their secrets?

I used to love finding
the initials people carved
into trees. Did they believe
that etching something
made it stronger or was it a way
of just saying: we were
once here?

5.

The largest forest I've ever gotten lost
in was the Superior National
and it is over three million acres of trees
but I was just a little off the path
and I have never been worried
in trees.

I used to dream of the woods
at night, how everything was darker,
how I couldn't see the places
I knew in the light,
but still I'd go deeper.

I have this recurring nightmare
now about forests on fire, I'm never
there but I see them on TV screens,
watch the limbs evolving into ash.

6.

Sometimes I wonder if I've asked enough
about the trees of your youth, if I've
tried to find where you keep
your stories,

but, I have a friend who doesn't miss
trees, likes the way that cities look
without them, so unbroken up, she
says, and I wonder what it's like
to not long for the shape
of limbs.

Some species of pine only
get regrown if a bird
breaks open their cones and spreads
the seeds somewhere else,
where some cones only open
under the heat of a forest
fire that melts their resin,
only regrow when
they are needed, born out
of loss. And these are
the things I like to tell
other people, but I don't
really know what I'm trying
to tell them.

7.

I want to write you a story
about trees
about the way that forests
in dreams
are places to get lost in

There's a tree I saw
alongside a road
and it looked like it was dying

but all its limbs
still reached up
for the sky
as if there was something
it still wanted
to be reaching for

In so many fairy tales,
our dead go into trees.
Maybe trees are always
liminal spaces, roots
beneath and arms above,
so easy to find the lost.

Last night, Houdini blessed me

in a dream. Handcuffed, and struggling, underwater, I saw no
escape. The sky through the water looked gray, pregnant with
rain. As a child, I studied men escaping, the way they moved
their bodies with such finely tuned precision. The body can be
a key. I worked my wrists the way I learned, one summer,
thinking one more skill would be all I'd need: pick a lock, slip
your hands from cuffs, false-cut a deck of cards. I had only a
few moments left my vision clouding like it does in video
games, after too many hits, and then the cuffs came away,
the surface came closer. Breaking up and out, I gasped air like
I couldn't remember what it was like to breathe. Houdini sat
on wooden chair, floating past me, and he reached out a hand,
placed it on my forehead, said
"everything will be alright." And though
I don't believe in dreams, just like Houdini taught me—
always be suspicious, it still felt
like something I could hold onto.

Cabinet Escape Tricks

"Rosabelle — answer — tell — pray, answer — look — tell — answer, answer — tell."
—Harry Houdini

Questions for Those Who Aren't Sure Where to Begin

Do you tell them your name? Just your name? Or a funny story about how it's always mispronounced, misspelled? Or about the nicknames you've held throughout your life? Your name is letters, is a word, should it be something else? How much of you is your name?

Do you make a joke after they tell you to take a deep breath in? Let it out. And again. And again.

And again.

How many of their yes/no questions do you answer yes? Remember not to lie, not to hedge, because this will matter later.

Do you tell it like a story? Or are you going to Dragnet it? Oh, wait, this reference becomes out of date. Do yours?

Is it just the facts?

What are "just the facts"?

Here, they are taking your pulse. They are counting the beats. Do you count with them?

When they say open up? Do you?

Or, wait, you're just supposed to say "ah."

Does it feel strange when they say you're fine/ they can't see anything wrong. Do you go quiet? Again?

And again.

The Escape Artist Wants To Tell You

Let me tell you about forgetting
it's easy enough to do.

I've forgotten to tell people
I loved them, at least

a dozen times and I've forgotten
the recipe for wild rice

stuffing, had to call my mom
and ask again, was it sage? Was

it something else?
What am I missing?

People forget their manners,
their exes, the color

of their grandmother's eyes,
that shade of not quite,

they forget so much
it could fill up the world

over and over
like the ocean

gets filled with things
we don't need.

I forget words sometimes
though that's a misfiring

of the brain, not really
a forgetting, more a temporary

misplacing, its as untreatable as the way
my heartbeat skips a step

when I think I might
one day forget you.

The other night I forgot the word
staying and so asked you if you'd reached

your destination of sleeping.
I wonder if you wondered

what I meant, so different than
you of careful words, you never

set them down
in the wrong spot

and I forget the word for staying
more often than I like

like I forget that I could
stay, and the thing about forgetting

is its easy
enough to do.

The Undue Acidity in Your Veins

The doctor tells us that I need
to learn how to cut into
my own skin

"If she can't do it now, she
won't be able to do it when
she has to." He says to you
and not to me.

He hands you the scalpel and
you place it in my hands and
you look me in the eyes and
you don't need to say
anything. So I place the tip

just above my kneecap, don't press
down, make a phantom cut up my thigh
in the same exact way you like to run a
fingertip up my skin under my skirt
under the table when you think no one is
watching my face.

The doctor says "Press" and
his voice is exclamations,
"Make her press" and you hold your
hand above my hand as you press into me
and I press into my skin until the blade
brings blood
and my throat thrashes out a howl

and the doctor says "good, good,
reward her." So you get on your knees to
lick the blood from my skin until the wound
closes.

Nociception

In the doctor's office, my body stretched
wary on the metal table

they take my pulse, press into my flesh,
say "tell me if it hurts yet"

and once when I was young, I snapped,
  with a popping sound like popcorn kernels
  in a booming speaker,
my Achilles' tendon, and the doctor said,
  "you should be crying,
  grown men cry from this,
  why aren't you crying?"

Pain has always hit me like a
pillow fort tumbling
onto my sleeping body

when the doctor points to a
chart from No Pain
to Worst Imaginable Pain

  a series of smiling faces whose upturned lips
  slowly collapse into grimace
I don't know how to chart
the feelings underneath my skin

I wonder how we learn to
talk about aching when all
of us speak
with different tongues

  sharp and stabbing and dull and throbbing
hoping that someone can translate our pain back to us

 and I tell the doctor
"I can't feel anything yet"

In Media Res

A friend once told me
that I was such a calm person,
it was good how steady
I stayed in emergency.

The truth is: I'm more
Hulk than meditative,
that my secret is I'm always
feeling catastrophic.

My skin holds mostly
worry underneath its layers,
so tightly coiled as to seem
still, like those guarded rattlesnakes

I don't know what step to untake
but I know which steps to avoid.

My body is always ready
to run, to catch, to save
but has a harder time
to settle, to want, to hold.

In moments of crisis—
the car crash, the hospital trip—
my hands stay steady, my mind
clears as if I have always been waiting

for this
As if
I will always be waiting for this.

Ends and Ends

The last woman to survive in a horror film
is called the Final Girl and the only
remaining member of a species gone extinct
is an endling. There's no word for the last
time you tell someone you love them
and mean it
but there should be.
In some other tongue, there might
be a word for the last sip
of a cup of coffee, or the last
bite of a cake. Would the word
change if the coffee is on the final
day of a vacation you took with the man
you loved before you both slipped from
one another's life? Or if the cake is from
a recipe from your great aunt—who died
in a war but no one in your family ever
says how as if war alone is answer enough.
The mathematician Fermat's last theorem
has no proof and now it's shorthand for something
inscrutable, for mystery. There should be a word
for your last thought and for your last act and isn't
there something extra sad about it when no one
understands them? There should be a word
for the last time you hold someone's hand.
There's a magazine that keeps sending me warning
last issues. I wonder if this is error or design. Or if
there's some alternate universe subscriber me
living in the world where last means never
means always.
Where you have your last issue,
last meal,
last kiss,
over and over.
Where your last I love you
is also the first
the best
And it happens

again and again
until we all survive.

Acknowledgments

Every book I write is a city, composed of the places I wrote each section and the people who helped, encouraged, and supported me. This book would not exist without Holly Walrath, and Interstellar Flight Press, whose passion for words helped craft these poems through the editorial process. I can't imagine a better press for this collection.

Thank you so much to every editor, staff member, and reader of the literary journals where these pieces originally appeared. Running literary journals is an often taxing, sometimes expensive, and always rewarding experience that requires dedication.

The past few years have been . . . challenging. So I also want to thank all of the friends who have been supportive, offered kindness, raged with me, or otherwise were (and are) awesome: Gillian Ramos, Kate Mead-Brewer, Hannah Grieco, Maegan Poland, Todd Dillard, Vance Kotrla, Carla Ferreira, Yohanca Delgado, M. Molly Backes, Marc Seals, Philippe Meister, Rita Mookerjee, Jordan Kurella, Zara Chowdhary, Ellie Gordon, Amy Barnes, Michael Tager, Chris Corlew, Tara Whitehead, Rachel Mans McKenny, Sara Doan, Crystal Stone, Samantha Kohnert, Maria Rago, Lisa Koca, Jennifer Fliss, Kanika Lawton, Ryan Dowdy, Kat Vo, Kelsey Hermann, and so many more who I am surely forgetting in the moment.

Finally I'm lucky to have people who make every day so much brighter. Sometimes it seems like a magic trick to be surrounded by so much good. Much love and thanks, which I will never be able to express enough, to: Erin Schmiel, Bronte Wieland, Matt Paul, Teo Mungaray, Hannah Cohen, E. Kristen Anderson, and Stephanie Gunn. To Brian Ramos and Mama, Papa, Gabe, Mike, Jack, Kimberly, Henry, Westley, Rowan, and Millie Hatch, with infinite love and thankfulness.

Grateful acknowledgment is made to the publications in which these poems first appeared:

Questions We Asked For Girls Turned to Limbs in *Uncanny*
Dissolutions in *Gamut*
Missing Girl Found in *Outlook Springs*
It's the Horror of My Friends that We Say Mean Things About Blondes in *Hypertrophic*
All Melusine's Daughters in *Rust + Moth*
The Detective, Years After and & Other Ways to Read the Dirt in *Abyss & Apex*
Once They Sainted a Mermaid in *Jersey Devil Press*
Apocalypse Scenario in *Moonchild*
You'd Be Home Now in *Graviton*
But Also This is Why the Robots Always Turn On Us and Other Words for Wanting in *Glass Poetry*
A Reward For You and the Ones I Don't Think You Need in *Occulum*
The Witch's House and Exposing Tricks in *Liminality*
Insert Bad Joke Here in *Gamut*
This Has All Happened Before in *New South*
We Who Vanish in *Prick of the Spindle*
He Was Always Almost Something in *Fogged Clarity*
When Everyone Else Says After in *Soft Blow*
Long in the Tooth in *Verse Wisconsin*
Cooking With Turmeric in *Boston Accent*
Lichenometry in *Alternating Current*
Cephalofoil in *Cease, Cows*
We Imagined Their Fossils to be Thunderbolts in *Bridge Eight*
Lacunae, Nociception, What the Earth Returns to Our Mouth, and Kitchen Piece in *Hobart*
There is No Matter in *Oxidant | Engine*
Questions for Those Who Aren't Sure Where to Begin in *Yes, Poetry*
The Undue Acidity in Your Veins in *Split Lip*
Ends and Ends and Questions for Men Falling Through Space in *Rabid Oak*

About the Author

Chloe N. Clark is the author of *Collective Gravities, Under My Tongue, Your Strange Fortune,* and *The Science of Unvanishing Objects.* Her forthcoming books include *Every Song a Vengeance* and *My Prayer is a Dagger, Yours is the Moon.* She is a founding co-EIC of literary journal *Cotton Xenomorph.* Her favorite basketball player will always be Rasheed Wallace and her favorite escape artist can only be Houdini.

About the Artist

Nana Masyuk-Frantsuzova graduated from the Saratov Art College.

"As a student, I found lines of the body were the best source of inspiration. That's the reason I take pictures of a lot of different people, who are beautiful in their own way."

Interstellar Flight Press

Interstellar Flight Press is an indie speculative publishing house. We feature innovative works from the best new writers in science fiction and fantasy. In the words of Ursula K. Le Guin, we need "writers who can see alternatives to how we live now, can see through our fear-stricken society and its obsessive technologies to other ways of being, and even imagine real grounds for hope."

Find us online at www.interstellarflightpress.com.

9 781953 736086